MY GRANDPA
SUPERMAN

By

Joyce McClanahan

This book is dedicated to a very special Grandpa and to all grandchildren who will see their own Grandpas as amazing people who have great stories to tell.

MY GRANDPA
PADDLES A CANOE

MY GRANDPA FLIES

MY GRANDPA GOES BACKPACKING

MY GRANDPA CLIMBS TREES

MY GRANDPA SAILS A BOAT

MY GRANDPA SWIMS

MY GRANDPA SKIS

MY GRANDPA CLIMBS MOUNTAINS

MY GRANPA DOES SCIENCE

MY GRANDPA READS

MY GRANDPA LOVES BABIES

MY GRANDPA COOKS

MY GRANDPA
GIVES DINGY RIDES

MY GRANDPA
HELPS WITH HAY

MY GRANDPA IS
SLEEPING. I LOVE MY
GRANDPA